Infinite Energy

Infinite Energy

Matthew Petchinsky

Infinite Energy: The Secret to Never Feeling Drained
By: Matthew Petchinsky

Introduction: Unleashing Infinite Energy

Imagine waking up every morning feeling completely rejuvenated, motivated, and ready to tackle whatever the day throws at you. Energy, in its true sense, is more than just physical stamina. It's the invisible force that fuels your mind, drives your emotions, and sustains your body. This book is about cultivating that boundless energy—what we call *infinite energy*—and applying it to every area of your life.

The Concept of Infinite Energy

Infinite energy isn't about chugging another cup of coffee or finding an extra hour of sleep, though those have their place. It's about creating a life where your mental, emotional, and physical resources are continually replenished rather than depleted. When you embrace the strategies in this book, energy becomes self-sustaining. You'll no longer experience the dreaded midday slump or the exhaustion that comes from juggling a hectic schedule. Instead, you'll tap into a reservoir of vitality that renews itself over time.

The Three Pillars of Energy

To understand infinite energy, you must first grasp its foundation: the three pillars that sustain it—mental, emotional, and physical energy.

1. **Mental Energy**

   Mental energy is your ability to focus, think clearly, and remain motivated. It's what helps you solve problems, make decisions, and pursue your goals. However, distractions, decision fatigue, and overthinking can drain this resource. This book will teach you how to declutter your mind, prioritize effectively, and keep your mental energy sharp throughout the day.

2. **Emotional Energy**

   Emotional energy is tied to your feelings, relationships, and sense of well-being. It's deeply influenced by how you process stress, handle setbacks, and engage with others. Toxic relationships, unresolved conflicts, or negative self-talk can sap this energy. You'll learn how to foster emotional resilience, practice gratitude, and build meaningful connections that uplift rather than deplete you.

3. **Physical Energy**

Physical energy is the foundation of it all. It's your stamina, vitality, and overall health. Proper nutrition, sleep, and movement are key, but so is understanding how to prevent burnout. By mastering the art of physical energy management, you'll feel strong, rested, and ready to handle any challenge.

When these three pillars are aligned and optimized, you create a synergy that fuels infinite energy. Neglect one, and the whole system begins to wobble. This book will help you find balance and harmony among the three.

Stories of Transformation

Let me share a few stories of people who have unlocked their infinite energy. Take Lisa, a corporate executive who once felt drained by her demanding job. She was on the verge of burnout until she learned to set boundaries, prioritize self-care, and practice mindfulness. Today, she not only excels at her work but also finds time to enjoy her hobbies and spend quality time with her family.

Or consider David, a college student who struggled with chronic fatigue due to poor sleep habits and constant stress. By incorporating small, manageable habits—like practicing a five-minute meditation before bed and eating energy-boosting snacks—he turned his life around and found himself excelling academically and socially.

These are just two examples of what's possible when you take control of your energy. Whether you're a busy parent, an entrepreneur, or someone simply looking to feel better every day, this book is for you.

What You'll Learn

Throughout this guide, you'll discover actionable strategies to:

- Identify and plug your biggest energy leaks.
- Build habits that energize rather than exhaust you.
- Cultivate emotional resilience and avoid energy-draining conflicts.
- Design a lifestyle that keeps your energy levels high, even during tough times.

Each chapter will build upon the last, offering insights, exercises, and tools to help you create a personalized plan for infinite energy. By the end of this book, you'll not only understand your energy better but also have the tools to transform your life.

So, are you ready to unlock the secret to never feeling drained again? Let's embark on this journey to infinite energy—your mind, body, and soul will thank you.

Chapter 1: Understanding Energy Leaks

Energy is the driving force behind everything we do. Yet, much of it slips away unnoticed, leaving us feeling depleted and wondering where it all went. Understanding where your energy is being drained is the first step to reclaiming it. This chapter explores the common sources of energy leaks, discusses their impact on your mental, emotional, and physical well-being, and introduces practical tools to help you identify and address these leaks.

Sources of Energy Drains in Daily Life

Energy drains are sneaky. They creep into your daily routine and, over time, take a toll on your vitality. Let's break down some of the most common culprits:

1. **Mental Overload**

   The constant barrage of information in the digital age overwhelms your mind. Endless notifications, emails, and multitasking lead to decision fatigue and a sense of being perpetually "on." This mental clutter prevents you from focusing on what truly matters and leaves you drained by the end of the day.

2. **Emotional Turmoil**

   Unresolved conflicts, toxic relationships, and negative self-talk sap emotional energy. Carrying the weight of anger, resentment, or insecurity can feel like dragging a heavy suitcase through your daily life. Emotional energy drains often go unnoticed until they manifest as irritability, anxiety, or a sense of disconnection.

3. **Physical Neglect**

   Poor sleep, unhealthy eating habits, and lack of movement are major energy drainers. When your body doesn't get the fuel, rest, and activity it needs, it struggles to keep up, leaving you feeling perpetually tired.

4. **Toxic Environments**

   Whether it's a demanding workplace, a chaotic home, or even an overstimulating digital space, your surroundings play a significant role in your energy levels. Toxic environments create stress and tension, which wear down your resilience over time.

5. **Unproductive Routines and Habits**

Overcommitting, procrastinating, or failing to set boundaries are examples of habits that drain your energy. These habits often stem from a lack of intention and awareness, but their cumulative impact can leave you feeling stuck in a perpetual cycle of exhaustion.

Mental Fatigue, Toxic Environments, and Unhealthy Habits

Let's take a closer look at how these specific drains operate and why they are so detrimental:

Mental Fatigue

Mental fatigue is the result of prolonged cognitive effort. Think about how exhausting it is to constantly make decisions, solve problems, or sift through endless streams of information. Every decision you make uses up a bit of your mental energy, and by the end of the day, you may feel like you've run a mental marathon. This is why even small, low-stakes decisions—like what to eat for dinner—can feel overwhelming when you're mentally fatigued.

How It Manifests:

- Difficulty focusing or concentrating.
- Forgetfulness or poor decision-making.
- Feeling unmotivated or apathetic.

Toxic Environments

Your environment significantly impacts your energy levels. A cluttered workspace, a noisy household, or a high-pressure office can create a constant undercurrent of stress. Even digital environments—like social media feeds filled with negativity—can drain your energy without you realizing it.

How It Manifests:

- Chronic stress or anxiety.
- Difficulty relaxing or feeling at peace.
- A sense of being "on edge" in certain spaces.

Unhealthy Habits

Habits like skipping meals, overindulging in caffeine, or spending hours on screens before bed disrupt your body's natural rhythms. These habits may seem insignificant in isolation, but their cumulative effect is a steady drain on your physical and mental energy.

How It Manifests:

- Persistent tiredness, even after rest.
- Irritability or mood swings.
- A sense of always "running on empty."

Tools to Identify Personal Energy Leaks

Now that we've identified the major sources of energy drains, the next step is to pinpoint which ones are affecting you. This requires self-awareness and reflection. Here are some tools to help:

Energy Leak Journaling

Start by keeping a daily journal where you track your energy levels throughout the day. Note when you feel most energized and when you feel the most drained. Pay attention to patterns. Are certain activities, people, or environments consistently depleting you?

How to Start:

- - Write down your energy levels on a scale of 1–10 at various points in the day.
    - Note what you were doing, who you were with, and how you felt emotionally and physically.
    - Review your entries at the end of the week to identify trends.

1. **Self-Assessment Checklists**

   Create a checklist of common energy drains and assess yourself honestly. For example:
   - Am I getting enough sleep?
   - Do I feel mentally overwhelmed or distracted?
   - Are my relationships uplifting or draining?

     This exercise can help you identify specific areas that need attention.

2. **Mindfulness Practices**
   Mindfulness can help you become more attuned to your energy levels in real time. Take a few minutes each day to pause, breathe, and check in with yourself. Ask, "How do I feel right now? What might be causing this feeling?" The simple act of noticing can help you make more intentional choices about how you spend your time and energy.

3. **Energy Mapping**
   Create an "energy map" of your day. Divide your day into blocks (e.g., morning, afternoon, evening) and list the activities in each block. Then, assign each activity a "+" (energizing), "-" (draining), or "=" (neutral). This visual representation can reveal how your time and energy are being spent.

Taking Action

By the end of this chapter, you should have a clear understanding of where your energy is being drained and the tools you can use to identify leaks. As we move forward, you'll learn how to address these drains and replace them with habits, environments, and practices that energize and empower you.

Remember, reclaiming your energy starts with awareness. Once you know where the leaks are, you can begin to patch them and set the stage for a life of infinite energy.

Chapter 2: The Power of Micro Habits

Big transformations don't come from massive overhauls overnight—they come from small, consistent actions that accumulate over time. Micro habits are the unsung heroes of sustainable energy management. These tiny, deliberate actions require little effort but deliver outsized results when practiced regularly. In this chapter, we'll explore how micro habits can help you maintain high energy levels, provide practical advice on hydration, nutrition, and movement, and delve into the science of habit stacking to maximize your energy gains.

Why Micro Habits Work

The beauty of micro habits lies in their simplicity. They are easy to start, require minimal time, and often fit seamlessly into your existing routines. For example, drinking a glass of water as soon as you wake up is a micro habit that boosts hydration and kickstarts your metabolism. Over time, micro habits compound, creating a ripple effect that enhances your physical, mental, and emotional energy.

The Ripple Effect of Micro Habits:

1. **Momentum:** Starting small builds confidence and momentum, encouraging you to adopt additional positive habits.
2. **Consistency:** Micro habits are easier to maintain, making them more likely to stick.
3. **Energy Balance:** Small, intentional actions reduce energy drains and replenish your reserves throughout the day.

As the saying goes, "Small hinges swing big doors." When it comes to energy, micro habits are the hinges that open the door to infinite vitality.

Practical Micro Habits for High Energy Levels

1. Hydration: The Energy Igniter

Water is the foundation of life—and energy. Even mild dehydration can lead to fatigue, headaches, and reduced mental clarity. By prioritizing hydration through simple habits, you can experience a noticeable boost in energy.

Micro Habits for Hydration:

- Drink a glass of water within 10 minutes of waking up.
- Carry a reusable water bottle and sip throughout the day.
- Set alarms or use apps to remind you to drink water at regular intervals.
- Add a slice of lemon, cucumber, or mint to your water for variety and added benefits.

2. Nutrition: Fuel for Your Body and Mind

Food is your body's fuel, but not all foods are created equal. What you eat directly impacts your energy levels. The key is to choose nutrient-dense, energy-boosting foods and avoid energy-depleting options like sugary snacks and processed meals.

Micro Habits for Nutrition:

- Start your day with a protein-rich breakfast to stabilize blood sugar levels.
- Keep healthy snacks like nuts, fruit, or yogurt on hand for quick energy boosts.
- Add a handful of greens to at least one meal a day.
- Prep your meals or snacks the night before to avoid last-minute unhealthy choices.

3. Movement: The Energy Generator

Movement is one of the fastest ways to recharge your energy. You don't need an intense workout to feel the benefits—small bursts of activity throughout the day can do wonders.

Micro Habits for Movement:

- Stretch for two minutes as soon as you get out of bed.
- Take a five-minute walk after meals to aid digestion and clear your mind.
- Perform a quick set of jumping jacks or push-ups during work breaks.
- Stand and move around while taking phone calls or brainstorming.

The Science of Habit Stacking

While micro habits are powerful on their own, combining them into a routine can supercharge their effectiveness. This concept is known as *habit stacking*—the practice of linking new habits to existing ones to make them automatic.

How Habit Stacking Works

Your brain craves familiarity and patterns. By attaching a new habit to an existing one, you piggyback on the momentum of an ingrained behavior. For example:

- Habit: Brushing your teeth.
- Stacked Habit: Doing 10 squats or calf raises while brushing your teeth.

This approach leverages your brain's natural tendency to follow established routines, making it easier to adopt new habits without additional mental effort.

Examples of Habit Stacking for Energy Gains:

1. **Morning Ritual:**
   - Existing Habit: Making coffee or tea.
   - Stacked Habit: Drinking a glass of water while the coffee brews.
2. **Work Routine:**
   - Existing Habit: Sitting down at your desk.
   - Stacked Habit: Writing down the top three priorities for the day before opening your laptop.
3. **Evening Wind-Down:**
   - Existing Habit: Watching TV or reading before bed.
   - Stacked Habit: Practicing deep breathing or gratitude journaling for five minutes.
4. **Meal Prep:**
   - Existing Habit: Cooking dinner.
   - Stacked Habit: Preparing a healthy snack for the next day while waiting for the food to cook.

By building these small actions into routines, you create a system that naturally maintains your energy levels without requiring constant motivation or willpower.

Making Micro Habits Stick

Consistency is key to reaping the benefits of micro habits. Here are a few strategies to ensure your new habits stick:

1. **Start Small:** Focus on one or two micro habits at a time. Trying to change too much at once can feel overwhelming.
2. **Track Your Progress:** Use a habit tracker or journal to monitor your efforts. Seeing your progress can be highly motivating.
3. **Celebrate Wins:** Reward yourself when you stick to your habits for a week or a month. Positive reinforcement strengthens your commitment.
4. **Be Flexible:** Life happens. If you miss a day or two, don't give up—simply pick up where you left off.

Energizing Your Day, One Habit at a Time

Micro habits may seem insignificant in isolation, but their cumulative effect is transformative. By focusing on small, manageable actions like staying hydrated, eating nourishing foods, and moving your body, you lay the foundation for sustainable energy. Habit stacking amplifies these efforts, making your energy-boosting routines seamless and automatic.

As you implement these micro habits, you'll notice a shift—not only in how you feel but in how you approach your daily life. Instead of battling constant fatigue, you'll have the energy to thrive. And the best part? These habits require no major overhauls or heroic efforts, just small, intentional steps that add up over time.

Chapter 3: Emotional Recharge Strategies

Emotions are powerful. They can energize us, filling us with passion and drive, or they can weigh us down, leaving us feeling drained and disconnected. Emotional energy, the fuel that powers our relationships, creativity, and resilience, is just as important as physical and mental energy. Yet, it's often overlooked or mismanaged. In this chapter, we'll dive into the profound impact emotions have on our energy levels, explore effective methods to release negative emotions, and introduce simple, actionable practices like gratitude journaling, mindfulness, and connection with loved ones to restore emotional vitality.

The Impact of Emotions on Energy Levels

Emotions are deeply intertwined with energy. Positive emotions such as joy, love, and excitement can uplift and invigorate us, while negative emotions like anger, frustration, and sadness can deplete our reserves. Here's how emotions influence energy:

1. **Energy Amplifiers (Positive Emotions):**
   Positive emotions create a ripple effect of high energy. They enhance mental clarity, improve physical stamina, and foster resilience. For example, feeling appreciated or loved can give you a boost that lasts for hours or even days.

2. **Energy Drainers (Negative Emotions):**
   Negative emotions consume energy. Anger, for instance, triggers a fight-or-flight response, releasing stress hormones like cortisol that sap physical and mental reserves. Sadness can feel like a heavy weight, slowing your movements and clouding your mind. Over time, unresolved negative emotions can lead to chronic fatigue, anxiety, and burnout.

3. **Energy Fluctuators:**
   Some emotions, such as uncertainty or worry, cause energy to fluctuate. These emotions can be particularly draining because

they keep you in a heightened state of alertness, waiting for a resolution that may not come.

Understanding the connection between emotions and energy is the first step to managing them effectively. The goal isn't to suppress or avoid negative emotions but to process and release them, allowing space for renewal and growth.

Methods to Release Negative Emotions

Releasing negative emotions is essential for maintaining emotional energy. Suppressing or ignoring them only compounds their effects over time. Here are some proven strategies for letting go of anger, frustration, sadness, and other energy-draining emotions:

1. Acknowledge and Name Your Emotions

The simple act of naming your emotions—"I'm feeling angry," "I'm feeling sad"—helps to disarm them. Research shows that labeling emotions activates the prefrontal cortex, the brain's rational center, reducing the intensity of emotional reactions.

How to Do It:

- Take a few deep breaths and ask yourself, "What am I feeling right now?"
- Write down your emotions in a journal or say them out loud to yourself.

2. Practice Emotional Release Techniques

Once you've identified your emotions, use physical or mental techniques to release them.

- **For Anger:** Engage in physical activity, such as punching a pillow, going for a run, or even tearing paper. Physical movement helps dissipate the pent-up energy of anger.
- **For Frustration:** Try deep breathing or progressive muscle relaxation. These practices calm the nervous system and shift you from a fight-or-flight state to a rest-and-repair state.
- **For Sadness:** Allow yourself to cry if needed. Crying is the body's natural way of releasing emotional tension and has been shown to reduce stress hormones.

3. Reframe Negative Thoughts

Negative emotions often stem from unhelpful thoughts or interpretations of events. By reframing these thoughts, you can change how you feel about a situation.

- **Example:** Instead of thinking, "I failed at this task," reframe it as, "This task didn't go as planned, but I learned something valuable."

Simple Practices for Emotional Recharge

While releasing negative emotions is crucial, it's equally important to proactively recharge your emotional energy. Incorporating these practices into your daily life can help you maintain emotional balance and resilience:

1. Gratitude Journaling

Gratitude is a powerful antidote to negative emotions. Focusing on what you're thankful for shifts your perspective from what's lacking to what's abundant.

How to Start:

- At the end of each day, write down three things you're grateful for.
- Be specific. Instead of "I'm grateful for my family," try "I'm grateful for the way my partner made me laugh today."
- Over time, this practice rewires your brain to notice and appreciate positive moments, boosting emotional energy.

2. Mindfulness Practices

Mindfulness helps you stay present, reducing the mental chatter and emotional turbulence that drain your energy. It's particularly effective for managing emotions like anxiety and frustration.

Simple Mindfulness Exercises:

- **Deep Breathing:** Spend five minutes focusing on your breath. Inhale deeply for a count of four, hold for four, and exhale for four.
- **Body Scan Meditation:** Close your eyes and mentally scan your body from head to toe, noticing and releasing any tension.
- **Five Senses Check-In:** Pause and notice five things you can see, four things you can touch, three things you can hear, two things you can smell, and one thing you can taste.

3. Connecting with Loved Ones

Human connection is one of the most effective ways to recharge emotionally. Sharing your thoughts and feelings with trusted friends or family members can provide comfort, perspective, and renewed energy.

Ideas for Meaningful Connection:

- Schedule regular check-ins with loved ones, even if it's just a quick phone call.
- Express appreciation for someone in your life. For example, send a heartfelt text or write a note.
- Spend quality time doing something you both enjoy, like cooking, walking, or watching a favorite movie.

Building an Emotional Recharge Routine

To maximize the benefits of these strategies, incorporate them into your daily or weekly routine. Here's an example of what an emotional recharge routine might look like:

1. **Morning:** Start the day with five minutes of gratitude journaling.
2. **Midday:** Take a mindful walk during lunch to release tension and refocus.
3. **Evening:** Reflect on your emotions, release any negative feelings through journaling or relaxation techniques, and connect with a loved one.

By consistently practicing emotional recharge, you create a buffer against life's inevitable stressors. Instead of reacting to challenges with frustration or fatigue, you'll approach them with clarity and resilience.

Emotional Energy: Your Hidden Superpower

Emotional energy is a renewable resource, but only if you actively manage it. By acknowledging and releasing negative emotions, practicing gratitude, cultivating mindfulness, and nurturing your connections with others, you can transform your emotional landscape. These strategies not only recharge your energy but also create a sense of peace and joy that sustains you through life's ups and downs.

Chapter 4: Unlocking Mental Energy

Mental energy is the foundation of productivity, creativity, and resilience. However, in today's fast-paced world, our mental resources are often stretched thin by cluttered thinking, decision fatigue, and constant distractions. Reclaiming your mental energy requires a deliberate approach to reducing cognitive overload and creating systems that promote clarity and focus. In this chapter, we'll explore the effects of cluttered thinking and decision fatigue, introduce techniques like time-blocking, prioritization, and meditation, and share cognitive hacks to help you maintain focus and avoid burnout.

The Burden of Cluttered Thinking and Decision Fatigue

Cluttered Thinking: The Mental Overload

A cluttered mind is like a cluttered room—it's harder to find what you need, focus on what matters, and feel at ease. Cluttered thinking arises from an overload of information, unresolved tasks, and constant distractions. It creates mental "noise" that makes it difficult to concentrate or think creatively.

How Cluttered Thinking Affects Mental Energy:

- Reduces your ability to process information efficiently.
- Increases stress and feelings of being overwhelmed.
- Impairs decision-making and problem-solving skills.

Decision Fatigue: The Energy Drain

Every decision you make—big or small—depletes a finite reservoir of mental energy. By the end of the day, even simple choices can feel overwhelming. Decision fatigue leads to procrastination, impulsivity, and poor decision-making.

Examples of Decision Fatigue in Action:

- Struggling to choose what to eat for dinner after a long day.
- Feeling paralyzed by options, even for minor decisions.
- Making rash choices because you're too mentally drained to deliberate.

Techniques to Boost Mental Clarity

Clearing mental clutter and conserving your decision-making power can dramatically improve mental energy. Here are practical techniques to help:

1. Time-Blocking: The Power of Structure

Time-blocking is a productivity technique where you schedule specific tasks during designated time slots. This method minimizes decision fatigue by reducing the number of choices you need to make throughout the day.

How to Implement Time-Blocking:

- **Step 1:** Identify your most important tasks (MITs) for the day.
- **Step 2:** Assign each task a specific time slot on your calendar.
- **Step 3:** Group similar tasks together (e.g., answering emails in one block).
- **Step 4:** Stick to the schedule, and avoid multitasking during a block.

Benefits of Time-Blocking:

- Provides a clear roadmap for the day, reducing mental clutter.
- Helps you focus on one task at a time, boosting efficiency.
- Limits procrastination by creating accountability.

2. Prioritization: Focus on What Truly Matters

Not all tasks are created equal. Prioritization involves identifying and focusing on tasks that have the greatest impact on your goals, while de-prioritizing or delegating less critical ones.

Techniques for Effective Prioritization:

- **The Eisenhower Matrix:** Categorize tasks into four quadrants:
    1. Urgent and important (do these immediately).
    2. Important but not urgent (schedule for later).
    3. Urgent but not important (delegate these).
    4. Neither urgent nor important (eliminate these).
- **Pareto Principle (80/20 Rule):** Focus on the 20% of tasks that produce 80% of the results.
- **Daily MITs:** Identify 1–3 high-priority tasks each day and complete them before anything else.

3. Meditation: Clearing Mental Clutter

Meditation is a powerful tool for enhancing mental clarity and reducing cognitive overload. Regular practice can help you quiet the mental chatter, improve focus, and boost overall mental energy.

Simple Meditation Practices:

- **Mindfulness Meditation:** Sit quietly and focus on your breath or a single point of attention. When your mind wanders, gently bring it back.
- **Guided Meditation:** Use apps or online resources to follow a guided meditation session.

- **Visualization:** Close your eyes and visualize yourself completing a task or achieving a goal with ease and focus.

How Meditation Boosts Mental Energy:

- Reduces stress and anxiety.
- Improves concentration and attention span.
- Enhances your ability to make thoughtful decisions.

Cognitive Hacks for Maintaining Focus and Avoiding Burnout

1. The Two-Minute Rule

If a task takes less than two minutes to complete, do it immediately. This prevents small tasks from piling up and adding to your mental clutter.

2. Chunking

Break large tasks into smaller, manageable chunks. This approach prevents overwhelm and allows you to focus on completing one piece at a time.

Example:

Instead of thinking, "I need to write a report," break it into smaller steps like:

1. Outline the main points.
2. Write the introduction.
3. Draft each section.
4. Edit and proofread.

3. The Pomodoro Technique

Work in focused intervals (typically 25 minutes) followed by a short break (5 minutes). After four intervals, take a longer break (15–30 minutes). This technique helps maintain focus while preventing burnout.

4. Digital Decluttering

Your digital environment plays a significant role in mental energy. A cluttered inbox or overwhelming social media feed can drain focus.

How to Declutter Digitally:

• Unsubscribe from unnecessary emails.
• Organize your desktop and folders.
• Set specific times for checking emails and social media.

- Use website blockers to minimize distractions during work hours.

5. Leverage Automation

Automate repetitive tasks to free up mental space.

- Use apps to automate bill payments or task reminders.
- Create templates for frequently used emails or documents.

6. Practice Mental Boundaries

Protect your mental energy by setting clear boundaries.

- Say no to commitments that don't align with your priorities.
- Limit exposure to negative news or toxic environments.

Building a Mental Energy Routine

To unlock and sustain mental energy, integrate the above strategies into a daily routine. Here's an example:

1. **Morning:** Begin with 5 minutes of mindfulness meditation to clear your mind.
2. **Work Hours:** Use time-blocking and prioritization to focus on high-impact tasks.
3. **Breaks:** Take Pomodoro-style breaks to recharge.
4. **Evening:** Reflect on your day using a simple journal and plan tomorrow's priorities.

Unlocking the Power of a Clear Mind

Mental energy is a renewable resource, but it requires active management. By reducing cluttered thinking, conserving decision-making power, and adopting strategies like time-blocking, prioritization, and meditation, you can unlock your mind's full potential. Incorporating cognitive hacks like the Pomodoro Technique, chunking, and automation will help you stay focused, avoid burnout, and maintain clarity throughout the day.

Chapter 5: Designing an Infinite Energy Lifestyle

The key to unlocking infinite energy lies not in isolated strategies, but in weaving the insights from mental, emotional, and physical energy management into a cohesive and sustainable lifestyle. A well-designed energy lifestyle empowers you to not only recharge your energy reserves but to thrive, even in the face of stressful periods or unexpected challenges. This chapter will guide you in creating a daily routine that integrates the practices discussed earlier and offer tips for customizing and adapting your plan to suit your unique circumstances.

The Infinite Energy Lifestyle: A Holistic Approach

Your energy lifestyle should address the three pillars of energy—mental, emotional, and physical—and create harmony among them. By balancing these components, you can establish a lifestyle that not only sustains energy but also enhances resilience, creativity, and well-being.

Key Principles of the Infinite Energy Lifestyle:

1. **Integration Over Isolation:** Practices for mental, emotional, and physical energy work best when combined. For example, mindfulness not only clears mental clutter but also soothes emotional turmoil.

2. **Consistency with Flexibility:** Small, consistent habits create long-term results, but flexibility ensures that the plan is sustainable even during challenging times.

3. **Proactive vs. Reactive:** Designing an energy lifestyle means addressing potential drains before they occur rather than scrambling to recover after the fact.

A Customizable Daily Energy Routine Template

The following routine incorporates insights from the previous chapters, providing a structure you can adapt to fit your needs.

Morning: Set the Tone

The first hour of your day sets the stage for the rest of it. Begin with practices that energize and center you.

1. **Hydration and Movement:**
   - Drink a glass of water immediately upon waking.
   - Spend 5–10 minutes stretching or doing light exercise to awaken your body.
2. **Mindfulness or Meditation:**
   - Spend 5–10 minutes in mindfulness meditation to clear mental clutter and focus your mind.
   - Alternatively, practice gratitude journaling by writing down three things you're thankful for.
3. **Plan Your Day:**
   - Review your priorities for the day, focusing on your top three tasks (MITs). Use time-blocking to allocate dedicated slots for these tasks.

Midday: Sustain Energy

The middle of the day is when many people experience an energy dip. Combat this with intentional practices.

1. **Nutrition and Hydration:**
    - Eat a nutrient-dense meal with a balance of protein, healthy fats, and complex carbs.
    - Continue drinking water or herbal tea to stay hydrated.
2. **Movement Breaks:**
    - Take a 5–10 minute walk or perform light stretching to refresh your body and mind.
3. **Mindful Pause:**
    - Spend 2–3 minutes practicing deep breathing or a quick body scan meditation. This helps recharge your mental and emotional energy.

Afternoon: Stay Productive

As the day progresses, focus on maintaining momentum while avoiding burnout.

1. **Focused Work:**
   - Use the Pomodoro Technique (25 minutes of focused work followed by a 5-minute break) for tasks requiring deep concentration.
2. **Emotional Check-In:**
   - Pause and assess how you're feeling. Are you carrying stress or frustration? If so, use an emotional release technique, such as journaling or talking to a trusted colleague or friend.
3. **Digital Detox:**
   - Limit distractions by turning off unnecessary notifications and closing unrelated tabs or apps during focused work periods.

Evening: Recharge and Reflect

The end of the day is a critical time to transition from activity to rest. Prioritize practices that promote relaxation and prepare your body and mind for restful sleep.

1. **Wind-Down Routine:**
   - Avoid screens for at least 30 minutes before bed. Instead, engage in calming activities like reading, journaling, or taking a warm bath.
2. **Gratitude Reflection:**
   - Write down three positive moments from your day, focusing on what went well and why. This shifts your mindset to positivity before sleep.
3. **Sleep Hygiene:**
   - Create a sleep-conducive environment by keeping your bedroom cool, dark, and quiet. Aim for 7–9 hours of quality sleep.

Adapting the Lifestyle During Stressful Periods

Life doesn't always go as planned. During periods of high stress or unexpected challenges, your energy needs and resources may change. Here are strategies for staying on track:

1. Scale Down, Don't Stop

During busy or overwhelming times, simplify your routine rather than abandoning it entirely. For example:

- If you can't do a full workout, take a 5-minute stretch break.
- If you're too tired for detailed journaling, write down one word or thought that reflects your day.

2. Focus on the Essentials

Prioritize the habits that have the greatest impact on your energy. For most people, these include:

- Staying hydrated.
- Getting at least 7 hours of sleep.
- Practicing mindfulness or gratitude for a few minutes each day.

3. Build in Recovery Time

Stress takes a toll on all three pillars of energy. Plan intentional recovery periods, such as a weekend spent unplugged from work or a daily 15-minute "reset" where you engage in something purely enjoyable.

4. Seek Support

Lean on your support system during challenging times. Whether it's asking for help with tasks, talking to a trusted friend, or seeking professional guidance, connection can lighten the load and recharge emotional energy.

Long-Term Tips for Energy Sustainability

To make your infinite energy lifestyle sustainable over the long term, keep these principles in mind:

1. **Track Your Progress:** Use a habit tracker or journal to monitor your energy levels and identify what works best for you.
2. **Adjust Seasonally:** Your energy needs may change with the seasons, workload, or life events. Periodically revisit and adjust your routine.
3. **Celebrate Milestones:** Acknowledge and reward yourself for maintaining your routine and achieving energy-related goals.

The Path to Infinite Energy

Designing an infinite energy lifestyle is about creating a rhythm that supports your mind, body, and emotions while allowing for flexibility. By integrating the strategies from this book—plugging energy leaks, building micro habits, recharging emotionally, and maintaining mental clarity—you create a system that powers you through life with resilience and vitality.

This is not just a plan for today or tomorrow but a lifestyle that evolves with you, helping you thrive in every season of life. With this foundation in place, you're well on your way to living with infinite energy.

Appendix A: Resources for Energy Mastery

This appendix is a comprehensive resource hub to support your journey toward infinite energy. It includes curated recommendations for books, apps, tools, guided meditations, fitness routines, productivity systems, and printable worksheets. These resources are designed to enhance your mental, emotional, and physical energy and help you integrate the strategies from this book into your daily life.

Books for Energy and Productivity

1. **Atomic Habits by James Clear**
   - A practical guide to building and sustaining positive habits through small, incremental changes.
   - Website: https://jamesclear.com/atomic-habits
2. **The Power of Now by Eckhart Tolle**
   - A transformative book on mindfulness and living in the present moment to reduce mental and emotional clutter.
   - Website: https://eckharttolle.com/power-of-now
3. **Deep Work by Cal Newport**
   - Explores the importance of focused, undistracted work for achieving peak mental performance.
   - Website: https://www.calnewport.com/books/deep-work/
4. **The Miracle Morning by Hal Elrod**
   - Offers a step-by-step guide to creating a powerful morning routine to set the tone for an energized day.
   - Website: https://miraclemorning.com/

5. **Mindfulness for Beginners by Jon Kabat-Zinn**
    ◦ Introduces foundational mindfulness practices to help recharge emotional and mental energy.
    ◦ Website: https://www.mindfulnesscds.com/

Apps to Boost Energy and Focus

1. **Calm**
    ◦ Features guided meditations, breathing exercises, and sleep aids to improve mental clarity and emotional balance.
    ◦ Website: https://www.calm.com/

2. **Headspace**
    ◦ A user-friendly app with mindfulness and meditation exercises for reducing stress and enhancing focus.
    ◦ Website: https://www.headspace.com/

3. **MyFitnessPal**
    ◦ Tracks your nutrition, hydration, and exercise to ensure optimal physical energy levels.
    ◦ Website: https://www.myfitnesspal.com/

4. **Forest**
    ◦ A productivity app that helps you stay focused by "growing" a virtual forest during uninterrupted work sessions.
    ◦ Website: https://www.forestapp.cc/

5. **Insight Timer**
    ◦ Offers free meditations and courses on mindfulness, sleep, and energy management.
    ◦ Website: https://insighttimer.com/

Guided Meditations for Energy

1. **Energy Boost Meditation by Tara Brach**
   - A short guided session to recharge your body and mind.
   - Link: https://www.tarabrach.com/meditation-energy/
2. **Mindful Energy Meditation on YouTube**
   - A free 15-minute guided meditation designed to enhance focus and restore energy.
   - Link: https://www.youtube.com/watch?v=ZToicY-cHIOU
3. **Morning Energy Meditation by Calm**
   - Available in the Calm app, this meditation sets a positive and energized tone for your day.
   - Website: https://www.calm.com/

Fitness Routines for Sustained Energy

1. **Yoga with Adriene (YouTube Channel)**
   - Free yoga sessions tailored for energy boosting, relaxation, and mindfulness.
   - Link: https://www.youtube.com/user/yogawithadriene
2. **7-Minute Workout App**
   - Offers quick, high-impact workouts to boost physical energy during busy days.
   - Website: https://7minuteworkout.jnj.com/
3. **Fitness Blender**
   - Provides free workout videos for all fitness levels, focusing on strength, endurance, and energy enhancement.
   - Link: https://www.fitnessblender.com/
4. **FitOn App**
   - A free app with workout plans and fitness classes designed to fit any schedule.
   - Website: https://fitonapp.com/

Productivity Systems

1. **Notion**
   - A versatile tool for planning, tracking, and organizing tasks and habits. Ideal for implementing time-blocking and habit tracking.
   - Website: https://www.notion.so/
2. **Trello**
   - A visual project management tool to organize tasks, track progress, and reduce mental clutter.
   - Website: https://trello.com/
3. **Todoist**
   - A task management app that prioritizes and schedules tasks for focused work sessions.
   - Website: https://todoist.com/
4. **Evernote**
   - A digital notebook for capturing ideas, notes, and to-do lists to keep your mind organized.
   - Website: https://evernote.com/

Printable Worksheets and Templates

1. **Energy Tracker Worksheet**
   - Track your energy levels throughout the day to identify patterns and energy leaks.
   - Download: Energy Tracker PDF
2. **Daily Routine Template**
   - Plan your day using time-blocking and prioritization. Includes spaces for MITs, hydration, meals, and mindfulness breaks.
   - Download: Daily Routine Template PDF
3. **Gratitude Journal Template**
   - A printable template for daily gratitude journaling to enhance emotional energy.
   - Download: Gratitude Journal Template PDF
4. **Stress Release Checklist**
   - A checklist of quick practices for releasing negative emotions and restoring balance.
   - Download: Stress Release Checklist PDF
5. **Habit Tracker**
   - A printable tracker to monitor the consistency of your micro habits.
   - Download: Habit Tracker PDF

Bringing It All Together

This curated list of resources is designed to empower you in maintaining infinite energy. Whether you're seeking inspiration, practical tools, or guided practices, these resources provide a strong foundation for sustaining physical, mental, and emotional vitality.

Remember, the key to mastering energy is consistency and adaptability. Use these tools to build and refine your routine, and revisit this appendix whenever you need a boost or a fresh perspective. By integrating these resources into your lifestyle, you'll continue to unlock and sustain the boundless energy that fuels a life of purpose and joy.

<u>Message from the Author:</u>

I hope you enjoyed this book, I love astrology and knew there was not a book such as this out on the shelf. I love metaphysical items as well. Please check out my other books:

-Life of Government Benefits

-My life of Hell

-My life with Hydrocephalus

-Red Sky

-World Domination:Woman's rule

-World Domination:Woman's Rule 2: The War

-Life and Banishment of Apophis: book 1

-The Kidney Friendly Diet

-The Ultimate Hemp Cookbook

-Creating a Dispensary(legally)

-Cleanliness throughout life: the importance of showering from childhood to adulthood.

-Strong Roots: The Risks of Overcoddling children

-Hemp Horoscopes: Cosmic Insights and Earthly Healing

- Celestial Hemp Navigating the Zodiac: Through the Green Cosmos

-Astrological Hemp: Aligning The Stars with Earth's Ancient Herb

-The Astrological Guide to Hemp: Stars, Signs, and Sacred Leaves

-Green Growth: Innovative Marketing Strategies for your Hemp Products and Dispensary

-Cosmic Cannabis

-Astrological Munchies

-Henry The Hemp

-Zodiacal Roots: The Astrological Soul Of Hemp

- **Green Constellations: Intersection of Hemp and Zodiac**

-Hemp in The Houses: An astrological Adventure Through The Cannabis Galaxy

-Galactic Ganja Guide

Heavenly Hemp

Zodiac Leaves

Doctor Who Astrology

Cannastrology

Stellar Satvias and Cosmic Indicas

<u>Celestial Cannabis: A Zodiac Journey</u>

AstroHerbology: The Sky and The Soil: Volume 1

AstroHerbology:Celestial Cannabis:Volume 2

Cosmic Cannabis Cultivation

The Starry Guide to Herbal Harmony: Volume 1

The Starry Guide to Herbal Harmony: Cannabis Universe: Volume 2

Yugioh Astrology: Astrological Guide to Deck, Duels and more

Nightmare Mansion: Echoes of The Abyss

Nightmare Mansion 2: Legacy of Shadows

Nightmare Mansion 3: Shadows of the Forgotten

Nightmare Mansion 4: Echoes of the Damned

The Life and Banishment of Apophis: Book 2

Nightmare Mansion: Halls of Despair

<u>Healing with Herb: Cannabis and Hydrocephalus</u>

<u>Planetary Pot: Aligning with Astrological Herbs: Volume 1</u>

Fast Track to Freedom: 30 Days to Financial Independence Using AI, Assets, and Agile Hustles

<u>Cosmic Hemp Pathways</u>

How to Become Financially Free in 30 Days: 10,000 Paths to Prosperity

Zodiacal Herbage: Astrological Insights: Volume 1

Nightmare Mansion: Whispers in the Walls

The Daleks Invade Atlantis

Henry the hemp and Hydrocephalus

10X The Kidney Friendly Diet
Cannabis Universe: Adult coloring book
Hemp Astrology: The Healing Power of the Stars
Zodiacal Herbage: Astrological Insights: Cannabis Universe: Volume 2
<u>Planetary Pot: Aligning with Astrological Herbs: Cannabis Universes: Volume 2</u>
Doctor Who Meets the Replicators and SG-1: The Ultimate Battle for Survival
Nightmare Mansion: Curse of the Blood Moon
<u>The Celestial Stoner: A Guide to the Zodiac</u>
Cosmic Pleasures: Sex Toy Astrology for Every Sign
Hydrocephalus Astrology: Navigating the Stars and Healing Waters
Lapis and the Mischievous Chocolate Bar

Celestial Positions: Sexual Astrology for Every Sign
Apophis's Shadow Work Journal: : A Journey of Self-Discovery and Healing
Kinky Cosmos: Sexual Kink Astrology for Every Sign
Digital Cosmos: The Astrological Digimon Compendium
Stellar Seeds: The Cosmic Guide to Growing with Astrology
Apophis's Daily Gratitude Journal

Cat Astrology: Feline Mysteries of the Cosmos
The Cosmic Kama Sutra: An Astrological Guide to Sexual Positions
Unleash Your Potential: A Guided Journal Powered by AI Insights
Whispers of the Enchanted Grove

Cosmic Pleasures: An Astrological Guide to Sexual Kinks
369, 12 Manifestation Journal

Whisper of the nocturne journal(blank journal for writing or drawing)

The Boogey Book

Locked In Reflection: A Chastity Journey Through Locktober

Generating Wealth Quickly:

How to Generate $100,000 in 24 Hours

Star Magic: Harness the Power of the Universe

The Flatulence Chronicles: A Fart Journal for Self-Discovery

The Doctor and The Death Moth

Seize the Day: A Personal Seizure Tracking Journal

The Ultimate Boogeyman Safari: A Journey into the Boogie World and Beyond

Whispers of Samhain: 1,000 Spells of Love, Luck, and Lunar Magic: Samhain Spell Book

Apophis's guides:

Witch's Spellbook Crafting Guide for Halloween

<u>Frost & Flame: The Enchanted Yule Grimoire of 1000 Winter Spells</u>

<u>The Ultimate Boogey Goo Guide & Spooky Activities for Halloween Fun</u>

Harmony of the Scales: A Libra's Spellcraft for Balance and Beauty

The Enchanted Advent: 36 Days of Christmas Wonders

Nightmare Mansion: The Labyrinth of Screams

Harvest of Enchantment: 1,000 Spells of Gratitude, Love, and Fortune for Thanksgiving

The Boogey Chronicles: A Journal of Nightly Encounters and Shadowy Secrets

The 12 Days of Financial Freedom: A Step-by-Step Christmas Countdown to Transform Your Finances

Sigil of the Eternal Spiral Blank Journal

A Christmas Feast: Timeless Recipes for Every Meal

Holiday Stress-Free Solutions: A Survival Guide to Thriving During the Festive Season

Yu-Gi-Oh! Holiday Gifting Mastery: The Ultimate Guide for Fans and Newcomers Alike

Holiday Harmony: A Hydrocephalus Survival Guide for the Festive Season

Celestial Craft: The Witch's Almanac for 2025 – A Cosmic Guide to Manifestations, Moons, and Mystical Events

Doctor Who: The Toymaker's Winter Wonderland

Tulsa King Unveiled: A Thrilling Guide to Stallone's Mafia Masterpiece

Pendulum Craft: A Complete Guide to Crafting and Using Personalized Divination Tools

Nightmare Mansion: Santa's Eternal Eve

Starlight Noel: A Cosmic Journey through Christmas Mysteries

The Dark Architect: Unlocking the Blueprint of Existence

Surviving the Embrace: The Ultimate Guide to Encounters with The Hugging Molly

The Enchanted Codex: Secrets of the Craft for Witches, Wiccans, and Pagans

Harvest of Gratitude: A Complete Thanksgiving Guide

Yuletide Essentials: A Complete Guide to an Authentic and Magical Christmas

Celestial Smokes: A Cosmic Guide to Cigars and Astrology

Living in Balance: A Comprehensive Survival Guide to Thriving with Diabetes Insipidus

Cosmic Symbiosis: The Venom Zodiac Chronicles

The Cursed Paw of Ambition

Cosmic Symbiosis: The Astrological Venom Journal

Celestial Wonders Unfold: A Stargazer's Guide to the Cosmos (2024-2029)

The Ultimate Black Friday Prepper's Guide: Mastering Shopping Strategies and Savings

Cosmic Sales: The Astrological Guide to Black Friday Shopping

Legends of the Corn Mother and Other Harvest Myths

Whispers of the Harvest: The Corn Mother's Journal

The Evergreen Spellbook

The Doctor Meets the Boogeyman

The White Witch of Rose Hall's SpellBook

The Gingerbread Golem's Shadow: A Study in Sweet Darkness

The Gingerbread Golem Codex: An Academic Exploration of Sweet Myths

The Gingerbread Golem Grimoire: Sweet Magicks and Spells for the Festive Witch

The Curse of the Gingerbread Golem

10-minute Christmas Crafts for kids

<u>Christmas Crisis Solutions: The Ultimate Last-Minute Survival Guide</u>

Gingerbread Golem Recipes: Holiday Treats with a Magical Twist

The Infinite Key: Unlocking Mystical Secrets of the Ages

Enchanted Yule: A Wiccan and Pagan Guide to a Magical and Memorable Season

Dinosaurs of Power: Unlocking Ancient Magick

Astro-Dinos: The Cosmic Guide to Prehistoric Wisdom

Gallifrey's Yule Logs: A Festive Doctor Who Cookbook

The Dino Grimoire: Secrets of Prehistoric Magick

The Gift They Never Knew They Needed

The Gingerbread Golem's Culinary Alchemy: Enchanting Recipes for a Sweetly Dark Feast

A Time Lord Christmas: Holiday Adventures with the Doctor

Krampusproofing Your Home: Defensive Strategies for Yule

Silent Frights: A Collection of Christmas Creepypastas to Chill Your Bones

Santa Raptor's Jolly Carnage: A Dino-Claus Christmas Tale

Prehistoric Palettes: A Dino Wicca Coloring Journey

The Christmas Wishkeeper Chronicles

The Starlight Sleigh: A Holiday Journey
Elf Secrets: The True Magic of the North Pole
Candy Cane Conjurations
Cooking with Kids: Recipes Under 20 Minutes
Doctor Who: The TARDIS Confiscation
The Anxiety First Aid Kit: Quick Tools to Calm Your Mind
Frosty Whispers: A Winter's Tale
The Infinite Key: Unlocking the Secrets to Prosperity, Resilience, and Purpose
The Grasping Void: Why You'll Regret This Purchase
Astrology for Busy Bees: Star Signs Simplified
The Instant Focus Formula: Cut Through the Noise
The Secret Language of Colors: Unlocking the Emotional Codes
Sacred Fossil Chronicles: Blank Journal
The Christmas Cottage Miracle
Feeding Frenzy: Graboid-Inspired Recipes
Manifest in Minutes: The Quick Law of Attraction Guide
The Symbiote Chronicles: Doctor Who's Venomous Journey
Think Tiny, Grow Big: The Minimalist Mindset
The Energy Key: Unlocking Limitless Motivation
New Year, New Magic: Manifesting Your Best Year Yet
Unstoppable You: Mastering Confidence in Minutes

If you want solar for your home go here: https://www.harborsolar.live/apophisenterprises/

Get Some Tarot cards: https://www.makeplayingcards.com/sell/apophis-occult-shop

<u>Get   some   shirts: https://www.bonfire.com/store/apophis-shirt-emporium/</u>

<u>Instagrams:</u>
@apophis_enterprises,
@apophisbookemporium,
@apophisscardshop
Twitter: @apophisenterpr1
Tiktok:@apophisenterprise
Youtube: @sg1fan23477, @FiresideRetreatKingdom
Hive: @sg1fan23477
CheeLee: @SG1fan23477

Podcast: Apophis Chat Zone: https://open.spotify.com/show/
5zXbrCLEV2xzCp8ybrfHsk?si=fb4d4fdbdce44dec

Newsletter: https://apophiss-newsletter-27c897.beehiiv.com/

If you want to support me or see posts of other projects that I have come over to: **buymeacoffee.com/mpetchinskg**
  I post there daily several times a day

Get your Dinowicca or Christmas themed digital products, especially Santa Raptor songs and other musics. Here: **https://sg1fan23477.gumroad.com**

Apophis Yuletide Digital has not only digital Christmas items, but it will have all things with Dinowicca as well as other Digital products.